I0187818

THE FANTASTIC BOOK OF TEACHER JOKES:
NOT JUST FOR TEACHERS

UNCONVENTIONAL
PUBLISHING

WWW.UNCONVENTIONALPUBLISHING.COM.AU

SHANE VAN

Copyright © 2023 Shane Van

ALL RIGHTS RESERVED. NO PART OF THIS BOOK IS TO BE REPRODUCED, COPIED OR USED IN ANY MANNER THAT IS NOT INTENDED FOR ITS PURPOSE WITHOUT THE WRITTEN PERMISSION FROM THE COPYRIGHT OWNER EXCEPT IN THE USE OF QUOTATIONS IN ARTICLES AND REVIEWS. FOR PERMISSION REQUESTS, CONTACT UNCONVENTIONAL PUBLISHING

ISBN – 978-0-6455601-7-6 HARD COVER

DISCLAIMER: THIS BOOK IS A WORK OF FICTION AND IS NOT TO BE TAKEN SERIOUSLY. THERE IS NOTHING IN THIS BOOK THAT SHOULD BE TAKEN AS FACT, ESPECIALLY SCIENTIFIC FACT.

TABLE OF CONTENTS

BAD STUDENTS

A teacher was pointing their ruler at a student.
"Class, at the end of this rod is a moron."
The student he is pointing to.
"Which end do you mean?"

I would have gotten an 'A' in all my exams if it wasn't for genetics. Now I am going to have to go home and tell my parents it's their fault I'm stupid.

I remember the time I brought home a report card with an A+ on it. When my parents looked at it and all they said was, "Who the hell is George? And you don't even do biology!!!!"

To the teachers that said, I would amount to nothing and be serving food at MacDonald's for the rest of my life. Fuck you!! Lucky Guess!!

Teacher: So you missed school yesterday?
Student: Actually, not at all.

What happened to the lazy student in military school?
He snapped to attention.

A biology teacher asked her class, "What is relative dating?"
"Isn't that when rednecks kiss their cousins?" replied one student.

What is the difference between a train and a teacher?
A teacher tells you to spit out the gum, but a train tells you CHEW CHEW CHEW!

A student was given detention for making chicken noises in class, they were using fowl language.

In a private school, the science teacher says to the class, "Did you know that protons have mass?"
"I didn't know they were Catholic," said a student.

A student kept annoying his physics teacher with questions about gravity. He was told to drop it.
Teacher: If you got $20 from 5 different people. What would you have?
Student: A new skateboard.

Teacher: Ok students, can anyone tell me the longest sentence they can think of?
Student: Sure, it's a life sentence.

Two students were arguing in geography class.

"What do you think is closer, Sydney or the Moon.?"

"The moon dumbass, you can't see Sydney from here."

Little Jimmy is handing in his biology assignment. The teacher starts browsing through it.

"Jimmy where is your appendix?" he asks.

"That is an easy one," Jimmy says as he lifts his stomach and points to his belly.

"Jimmy, what is a specimen?" the teacher asks.

"That's an easy one Miss. An Italian astronaut."

Biology teacher: If you don't stop making puns about plants, I will send you outside.

Student: Don't worry I'm leafing.

The biology teacher handed back the exams on insects. Little Jimmy had received an 'F'.

"Are you chitin me?" he says to the teacher.

"Me biology teacher told me all ants are females!" said little Jimmy to his mum.

"Oh is that so?" asked his mum with a curious look on her face.

"Yeah, the males are called uncles!" Jimmy continues.

A chemistry professor has a beaker of solvent. He pulls out a $50 note and puts it in the beaker. He turns to the class and asks,

"Will this $50 dissolve?"

Jimmy answers, "No, Sir."

"Excellent, Jimmy. Can you tell me why?"

"Because you're too much of a tight ass to dissolve $50."

There are three students, one is studying physics, another mathematics and the last one engineering. They are each given a ball and told to find the volume.

The maths student measures its diameter and from there, works out the volume.

The physics student immerses it in water to find the volume. The engineering student starts spinning it around like crazy trying to find the model number.

A physics teacher once told me that the only way I would pass was if pigs fly. I studied really and developed my own experiment for which I got expelled. I believe I was set up since it was never specified that the pigs had to fly of their own accord.

Why did the pupil eat his homework?

Because the teacher said it was a piece of cake.

Why did the kid cross the playground?
To get to the other slide.

Teacher: I thought I told you to stand at the end of the line!
Student: I tried but someone was already there.

Teachers are always telling me how great my work is, how outstanding it is. The funny part is I haven't even handed it in yet.

Why did a student take a ladder to school?
It was his first day of High School.

Worse Teachers

What do you get when you cross a vampire with a teacher?
Blood tests.

A teacher would often start the lesson off with a joke they got from Reddit. They had the day off so a subreddit.

What is the difference between a teacher and a large pizza?
A pizza can feed a family of four.

Teachers deserve a lot of credit, but if we got paid more, maybe we wouldn't need as much bank credit... Just saying.

There was a plan to start arming teachers. The librarians were going to get silencers.

Did you hear about the student that got a detention for talking about drugs?
The teacher made them stay back and do lines.

The strictest teacher at my school was Mr Turtle. Weird name but tortoise well.

Why was the cross-eyed teacher fired?
He couldn't control his pupils.

What do you call the teacher who forgets to take roll call?
Absent-minded

A quite talkative student was asking the biology teacher, several questions to try and get a rise out of them.
Student: So, if a snake bites me and I die, would that be called venomous?
Teacher: Yes, Johnny the snake is venomous
Student: What if I bite the snake and it dies?
Teacher: Then you're venomous
Student: What if the snake bites me and someone else dies?
Teacher: That is correlation and causation
Student: What if the snake bites itself and I die?
Teacher: That is called voodoo
Student: What if the snake and I bite each other and neither of us dies?

Teacher: Then you're into weird kinky shit and probably going to hell.

What do you call a teacher that doesn't fart in class?
A private tooter.

Time is the best teacher of all. Time kills all its students.

What did the teacher say to the ghost student?
Look, I am going to go through this one more time.

Student: Chemistry is hard.
Teacher: Yeah so is life, get over it.

What is a teacher's favorite Country?
Expla-nation.

What do you call a teacher without their students?
Happy.

Why was the teacher wear sunglasses in class?
The students were too bright.

My attempts at a teaching career.
I started teaching history but that's in the past.

I tried teaching chemistry but there were elements I couldn't understand.

I tried teaching biology but my heart wasn't in it.

I didn't like teaching math, something wasn't adding up.

I couldn't teach German, I was the wurst.

I am now trying physics. Apparently it has potential.

Jesus was in front of a crowd on the mountain side.

Surrounded by his disciples he began teaching them.

"Blessed are the poor in spirit, for theirs is the kingdom of heaven."

"Excuse me Jesus, I didn't bring a pencil" interjected Mark.

"Will there be a test? Will this be on?" cried out James.

Just as this was occurring a group of Pharisees walked up to Jesus and interrupted.

"Excuse me, but do you have a lesson plan? Did you communicate the learning objective and have it clearly displayed to all students? Have you differentiated the topic material for all cognitive levels and considered any medical shortcomings? Would you mind if I unobtrusively sat in your class and tally how many different learning strategies you use and how many Positive Behavior for Learning interactions are you doing with your class?"

I remembered back at school; our Principal once suspended a friend of ours for illegally downloading some Nickelback songs. They actually expelled a student who purchased it.

I could sit here all day and explain quantum physics, but you wouldn't understand a thing. It's not that you're dumb, it's just I am a really crappy teacher.

Student askes their physics teacher if they could go to the bathroom.
"Sure," he says, "Liquid, Solid or Gas?"

When I was teaching, the school let me go because I gave a student a detention for being too "tardy". In hindsight, special education probably wasn't for me

One morning, a mother walks into her son's room and pulls back the curtains.
"Ok, rise and shine, you have to get ready for school," she announces merrily.
"I don't want to!" he yells pulling the cover back over his head.
"Why on earth not dear?" she asks soothingly.
"All the kids hate me, the teachers all pick on me, and I have no idea what I am doing."

"Well dear, you have to go! For starters, you're a 49-year man and the school Principal!!"

In a school, the agriculture department needed to build a fence around some sheep. A manual arts teacher, a science teacher and the senior physicist's teacher go to the plot to map out the area. The manual arts teacher just looks at the material and builds a simple square fence without any fuss.

The science teacher starts pulling it down.

"No, no, no," he says. "I know how to maximize the space for the material."

So, the science teacher starts building a circle fence.

The physicist, pipes in, "Let me show you how to do it."

He then grabs a material and builds a tiny fence around himself.

"See, now I will quantify myself as the outside."

Shocking Parents

My wife and I decided to make a pact, that we would make a list of all the people who could sleep with if we got a chance. She chose, Chris Hemsworth, Channing Tatum, Peirce Brosnan, and Zac Efron. I chose her sister, her cousin that was at our wedding, the local bar girl and our son's teacher.

I heard the best geography joke the other day. You wouldn't get it, you had to be there.

Little Jimmy went to school and was sitting in anatomy class. The teacher was busy using a poster was pointing out the reproductive parts of the male. Little Jimmy starts to get confused and raised his hand.
"Miss, Miss, that's wrong. My Dad has 2 penises!"
"That's not possible." replied the teacher.
"My daddy has a small one to pee with and a long one to brush my mom's teeth with!"

During a bonding session, a son is asking his father all sorts of questions, covering almost every topic imaginable.
"Dad, what is String theory?", the young man asks.

"Why are you asking me such difficult questions, can't you just ask me something a lot easier?" The father replies.

"Ok, so dad why is mum always yelling at you?"

"Ok Son, you see String theory is a framework from particle physics……"

I failed science and school, so to get back at my teachers I named my son physics. Now when the school calls me, they say. "Is this Tom, the father of Physics?"

What is the difference between leaving detention and driving a Kia?

You feel like less of a dick when you leave detention.

A teacher explains to her students what morals are. She gives an example and for homework, she sets the task that the kids have to go home and ask their parents for an example of a story that has a moral.

The next day the students are back, and school and they are all giving their stories with little Susie being the last student.

"My dad told me a story, about mum when she was younger," she says.

"You see mum was a combat medic for the marines, she was always jumping out of chinooks patching guys up under fire or busy shooting at them from the side of the helicopter. Then one day the chinook was hit by an RPG, and it started going down, so mum bailed with a parachute. She only had a bottle of whiskey which she used to give to troops, her combat knife and a 9mm pistol. Seeing that she was going to land in the middle of 16 Taliban fighters, mum decided to guzzle the whiskey. When she landed, she shot 13 of the troops and stabbed the last 3."

The room was deafly silent.

"Um, Susie, what was the moral of that story?" asks the teacher after a few moments.

"Oh, Dad said, don't fuck with mum when she's pissed."

A young boy comes home from school and goes to his dad.

"Hey dad, my math teacher wants to see you."

"Why?" he asks.

"Well, I was in class and the teacher asked me, what is 4 x 6? I said 24. He then asked me, ok now what is 6 X 4? I said well, what is the fucken difference?"

"Yeah, well what is the difference?" said the father, "I will go and see him."

A few days later the boy comes home and goes straight

to his dad.

"Hey dad, did you speak to the math teacher yet?"

"No, I haven't!" said the dad.

"Well dad, now you gotta see the gym teacher, as well."

"What for?" The dad says.

"Well, we are in the Gym, and we are holding onto ropes, He tells me to lift my right leg, so I do, and then he tells me to lift my left. I then said how do you want me to stand? On my cock?"

"I don't get it how are you meant to stand? I will have to talk to him." said the boy's dad.

A few days later, the boy comes home really upset, and the kid's father sees it.

"Hey son, sorry I haven't had a chance to go and talk to your teachers yet."

"Don't bother dad, I go expelled today."

"What happened?" said the father mortified and angry.

"Well, I was asked to go the Principal's office, when I got there, the Principal, maths, gym and art teacher, were waiting for me."

"What the fuck was the art teacher there for?" interrupted the dad, angrily.

"That's exactly what I said.!!"

Little Jimmy

Teacher: "How much is half of 8?"

Little Jimmy: "Well miss do ya mean up or down or across?"

Teacher: "I am sorry Johnny but what are you talking about?"

Little Jimmy: "Well you see miss, if I cut it up and down, I get 3 and a capital E, but across I get 0."

After the school holidays, the students all come back to school and share what they did during the holidays. Each student got up and told the class about their adventures and the teacher asked 1 or 2 questions.

When it was little Jimmy's turn, he stood in front of the class and the teacher asked what he did for the holidays. "I went to my Uncle Johnny's farm. I was there for a week." said little Jimmy.

"Can you give us some examples of farmyard noises?" asked the teacher.

So Little Jimmy cupped his hands together and started yelling out.

"Close, the Fucken gate, Stop chasing the Fucken Chickens. Get the Fuck off that Dickhead!!"

Little Jimmy failed his biology exam. When asked; "What are inside cells?" His answer, "My Daddy and Uncle Jimmy" wasn't quite right.

A biology teacher asks her class.
"Ok class, what separates the head from the rest of the body?
Little Jimmy yells out, "An axe Miss"

Young Jimmy comes home from school and his mum asks him, "What did you learn at school today."
"Today we learned about electricity, Ohm my gawd it was awesome."

Little Jimmy comes home all happy and excited.
His mum asks him, "How was school, honey?"
"Great mum, today we learnt about explosive chemicals in chemistry class," Jimmy replied.
"Oh, that's a bit concerning, so what are you learning at school tomorrow?"
"What School?"

In chemistry class, the students were given an assignment of studying chemical reactions and recreating one. As the students were mixing various chemicals, some making hydrogen gas and popping them, others creating endothermic reactions, the teacher was walking around helping students. He notices little Jimmy who never studies, about to put 1kg of potassium into water. "Ah Jimmy, you need to stir the water for 5 mins first." says the teacher.

"Why Sir?" asks Jimmy.

"It will give me a chance to get the hell out of here first."

A science teacher asks the class, "I have 2 liquids, I have water and butane. What would be a good measurement of liquids?"

"Please sir, I would use litres." Shouts our little Jimmy.

"Very good Jimmy, now class which one is heavier?"

"The butane," shouts out Jimmy again, "because it's a lighter fluid."

The teacher wanted to do a quick spelling test around the classroom.

"Ok class, I am going to select a letter from the alphabet, and you will have to give me a word that starts with that letter and say it in a short story," she mentions.

A lot of the kids start putting up their hands, including

Little Jimmy. The teacher knew that Little Jimmy did swear too much and was very inappropriate, so she was busily trying to avoid him.

"Ok, Susie can you give me a word that starts with b.?" he said.

"B for birds." Susie said.

"Ok, now give me the word birds in a short sentence," he said

"When I woke up this morning, lovely little birds were singing at my window."

This went on for quite a while and Little Johnny had his hand up the whole time, his face was almost turning purple to stop himself from yelling out. In the end, the teacher felt sorry for him and gave him a chance.

"Jimmy, can you give me a word that begins with C?"

"Contagious Sir," Jimmy replies.

The teacher let out a sigh of relief.

"Ok, Jimmy now give me a story using the word contagious."

"Well, Dad was driving me to school today, and we were stuck behind a truck carrying pumpkins. The driver went too fast around the corner and the whole truck tripped over and pumpkins spilled out. Then dad says, that will take the contagious to clean up."

Little Jimmy is at school, in class just watching the clock, counting down the minutes for lunch. The teacher turns around and says, "Ok class, I will give you 3 quotes, if you get one you can get who said it then you can go early to lunch."

"Who said, 'We shall fight them on the beaches?' "

Little Jimmy is straining and thinking when someone at the back of the room yells out, "Winston Churchill!"

"Very good, you may go," she says to the student.

"Now who said, 'Imagination is everything… it is the preview of life's coming attractions?' "

Once again Little Jimmy is racking his brain when across the other side of the room someone yells out. "Miss that's Einstein."

"Very good, you can go early to lunch."

"Ok class, now who said, 'I have a dream!' "

Immediately someone yells excitedly, "Miss, Miss, Martin Luther King, Miss, Miss."

"Yes, you can go."

Little Jimmy, angrily says, "Them Bitches need to Shut Up!!"

"Who said that!", said the teacher turning around.

"Oh, Miss. It's Bill Cosby, can I go now?"

One day the teacher during a maths lesson asks, "Ok Jimmy, 3 birds are sitting on a fence and you shoot one, how many birds are left?"

"Oh Miss, none, 'cause the other birds flew away!" said Little Jimmy.

"No, Jimmy, there are 2 birds left because they flew away somewhere but I like the way you think" the teacher replies.

"Ok Miss now, let me ask you a question. 3 women are in a shop having ice cream. One is eating the ice cream, one is licking the ice cream and one is sucking the ice cream. Which one is married?" Little Jimmy blurts out.

The teacher rolls her eyes, "Ok Jimmy, the one sucking the ice cream?"

"Nah miss, it's the one with a wedding ring on her finger, but I like the way you think."

Little Jimmy got detention for being rude. The teacher had told the class that they will be watching a documentary on drugs.

Little Jimmy yelled, "That's awesome Miss, so what's the doco going to be on?"

Primary Years

What did one eye say to the other eye?
I don't know about you but something between us smells.

Why do bubbles hate school?
They don't do well with POP quizzes.

What did the crayon say to the pencil?
What's your point?

What is the king of the classroom?
The ruler

Why did the magician fail his exam?
He only got the trick questions right.

A primary teacher was teaching the class biology. She was saying to her class that humans are the only animal to stutter.

Little Jimmy puts up her hand, "Miss, miss that's not true. My neighbour's cat stuttered once."

"I am sorry Jimmy, that's not possible."

"Yeah miss, it's true. It jumped into our yard and our Rottweiler saw it. Then the cat started going fffft fffft fffft and before the cat could tell it to fuck off, the dog ate him."

A student asked the teacher, "Miss how do stars die?"

"Generally, with a drug overdose." she replied.

What was the name of the teacher that was always late to school?

Mister Bus.

A teacher came to class and started throwing cotton wool at all students.

"Ok students, I want you to put it in just 1 ear, you can choose which."

"Why miss?"

"Because whatever I say usually goes in one ear and then out the other."

Student: Hey do you want to hear a joke?

Teacher: Sure, since I am looking at one.

Why did the teacher write the classroom rules on the window?

They want their instructions to be clear

What are the 10 things a Kindergarten teacher can always count on?
Her fingers.
What are the 9 things a kindergarten teacher can always count on?
Her fingers, after an incident she had with the automatic pencil sharper.

Which teachers love to grow plants?
Kindergarden teachers.

A teacher was supervising a school camp for a week when on day one a student wandered off and fell into a well. The teacher dutifully calls the parents to tell them what's going on.
"Hi. Mr and Mrs Smith, I need to tell you that Little Jimmy fell down a well."
"Omg is he ok?" cried the worried parents.
"I think so, he stopped asking for help yesterday."

Higher Stuff

Why did the music teacher hand out ladders to students?
So, they could hit the high notes.

Did you know about the student that got detention in art class?
He said he was framed.

Why was the music teacher sad?
He had a lot of trebles.

What do you get when Johann Sebastian Bach falls off a horse but then gets back on again?
Bach in the saddle again.

I heard the music teacher sing to the class today, I then suggested that next time I could be a tenor. Tenor twelve meters away from their room.

What do you call it when a musician is erasing their own music?
Decomposing

My music teacher just composed a piece on heterosexual killer whales. He did have trouble finding a conductor that knew how to orca straight.

A horse is listening to the radio one day and hears a rock song. The horse falls in love with it and decides it wants to learn how to play the guitar and goes to find a music teacher. Sure enough, he finds one and rings the music teacher up.

"Hi, can you teach me to play the guitar?" asks the horse.

"Sure, I can, that's easy, I can teach anyone to play," says the music teacher.

"Just to let you know I am a horse so it might be difficult for me."

"I mean I can teach any person or any animal to play," said the music teacher.

And the teacher did just that. He taught the horse how to play the guitar perfectly. One day as the horse was playing, a rooster was walking past the stable and hears it.

"Wow that's amazing do you mind if I jam with you?" asked the rooster.

"Of course not," said the horse, "What instrument do you play?"

"None, but I would love to learn the keyboard."

"I know the perfect music teacher for you, he can teach any person and animal."

So, the horse called up the music teacher and the music teacher agreed to teach the rooster. It took a few months but the rooster became perfect at the keyboard.

The horse and the rooster were busy jamming when the horse stopped.

"We are slightly out of beat. We need a drummer." said the horse.

"Why don't we ask the cow?" said the rooster.

"Hey cow," said the horse, "Would like to join us and make a band? We need a drummer." Yelled out the horse.

"I would love to," said the cow, "But I don't know how to play the drums."

"That's easy! We know this great music teacher. He can teach any person or any animal how to play any instrument" said the rooster.

They called the music teacher up, and just as before the music teacher agrees and the cow now knows how to play the drums expertly.

During another jam session, they stop and start talking.

"This band is missing something," said the cow.

"I know a bass guitarist. Imagine if we get one, we would be a real band and maybe even do gigs!!!" said the horse excitedly.

"How about I go and ask the dog?" says the rooster.

Just like before the dog agrees to play for the band and the same music teacher agrees to teach the dog and the dog learns how to play the bass guitar perfectly.

They are jamming one day when the music teacher decides to film them and puts the video on YouTube. They are an overnight viral sensation, the next second they are getting record deals and planning a tour date.

As they are about to set off on the tour date and they are all aboard the bus, the horse gets a message that his grandma is sick. He apologizes to the band and says he will meet them at the first venue in Las Vegas, but he has to go.

Unfortunately, when he gets to his grandma's farm, she has already passed away. With a heavy heart, he decides he still needs to play with his band, they are like his family now and he can't let them down. So, he races off to Las Vegas.

When he gets to Las Vegas, there is only the music teacher standing there with a sad look on his face.

"Hi, I tried to call you as there is something I must discuss with you. The bus rolled over on the highway, and everyone is dead. No one survived." Said the music teacher.

The horse was in shock. He didn't know what to do or where to go. He just started wondering about the streets in Las Vegas. He eventually stumbled into a club and walked up to the bar. The barman looked at him and yelled "Hey why the long face?"

The music teacher had to call home for Little Jimmy
"Hi, I think we have a young Elvis on our hands." said the teacher.
"Why? Is he a great singer?" asked the parent.
"No, we found him dead on the toilet."

Why wasn't the music teacher upset after his car accident?
The damage only seemed to B minor.

Where did the music teacher lose their keys?
In the piano.

What is a music teacher's favorite saying?
F you guys

What was the name of the music teacher's dog?
Sub-woofer.

Fred Mercury was busy taking a tour of a school when he was introduced to the music class.

"What instrument do you play?" asked the music teacher.

"The audience!" replies Freddie.

"What do you mean, the audience?" asked the teacher.

"AAAAAAAYYYOOOOOOOO" sang Freddie.

"AAAAAAAYYYOOOOOOOO" the whole class sang back.

A music teacher was asking questions of the class, when one of the students answered, "Justin Bieber and Miley Cyrus".

"No, no, no. I said sheet music." replied the teacher.

What was the Pirate's favorite subject at school?
Arrrrrtttt.

When I was in music class, I would always walk past the drums and just hit them. The music teacher told me if I did it again I would get into trouble. So, I hit them again. He was right. There were some serious repercussions.

During Music class, Johnny Gambino, nephew to Al Capone walks into music class carrying his violin. The class all sit down and start unpacking their musical instruments. Johnny opens his violin case and pulls out a Tommy gun to the screams of the rest of the students. When little Johnny looks at the gun and starts laughing manically.

"Why are you laughing?" asks the teacher, hiding under his desk.

"Oh, I am just thinking about the look on my uncle's face when he goes to the bank this afternoon."

In art class, I painted a self-portrait. My art teacher said it looked terrible but they also said it was extremely realistic and lifelike.

"Why are you staring at a blank piece of paper?" asked the art teacher.

"I am drawing a blank" replied the student.

Did you hear about the fight between the art teachers?
They drew blood.

Why do Nazis make horrible art teachers?
They don't like mixing colors.

Everyone knows who Leonardo da Vinci is, the famous scientist and artist, but not everyone knows the story of his dad at parent-teacher interviews.

The first teacher he meets is the maths teacher and greets him with, "Good evening fir, how if my fon working in you claff?"

The teacher realizes that he must have a speech impediment and decides to politely ignore it.

"Your son is fantastic and an absolute treasure to teach. I wish all my students were like him. He understands everything on the first try and you should see some of his work in geometry." replies the maths teacher.

Leonardo's dad just beams with pride.

"You fhould fee him at home, he if alwayf working profectf." says the father.

The next visit is to the science teacher and he asks the same questions as before.

"Your son is amazing, he is bright, and he has an amazing grasp of biology." says the science teacher.

"Oh fes, he if alwayf catching fmall birdf and lizardf. Then he difectf to fee the anatomy."

The next teacher he sees is the art teacher, who jumps out of their chair to greet the father.

"You must be Leonardo's father! Your son is a real talent, he will go far. All his pictures are so life-like, so real. They are better than anything I will ever be able to create!"

"I know," said the father, "the other day the affhole painted puffy on the ftove."

An English teacher was pulled into a hospitality class as a cover.

"Ok students today we are going to bake synonym rolls, just like grammar used to make."

The electrics teacher was a bit obsessed with the woke movement, he kept talking about the trans-sisters.

Why did margarine end up in detention?
All the butter students turn up to class on time.

A fight broke out between the manual arts teacher and PE teacher.

Yeah, the PE teacher was super fit, benched 200 pounds and was a black belt in Judo. But a hammer is still a fucking hammer!

A student was struggling with a mapping exercise.

"I will never get this!" grumbles the student.

"Not with that latitude" answers the geography teacher.

My grandfather went down in history, he also got a hand job in geography… allegedly.

Why do paper maps never win at poker?
Because they always fold.

Why do geography teachers find mountains so funny?
Because they are Hilarious.

A teacher asked one of their students.
"Dayna, can you please point to America on this world map?."
"Sure," she says and correctly points to where the country is located.
"Ok Dayna, can you tell me who discovered America?"
"Sure, it was me."
The main 2 things I learned from online dating; geography and disappointment.

A geography teacher was teaching his class how to read maps. He explained about latitude, longitude, degrees, which ones go first, and where they are located on a map. He then asked his students: "What if I asked you to meet at 345 Northings and 743 Eastings?"

After a moment of silence, one brave student puts up their hand "Um I think you would be eating alone."

The Australian convicts came across on the first fleet.
The Pilgrims arrived in America on the Mayflower.
What did the teachers sail on?
Scholarships

Did you hear about the history teacher?
He liked to Babylon.

A history teacher had some issues getting over their ex, so they went to see a counsellor for help. It turns out they were living in the past.

Sporting Coaches

Hot Tip! Physical Education is not when you beat your kids, for doing something wrong.

I remember 1 bit of advice my gym teacher gave me. "Push with your legs, the power comes from your legs." I suppose that was bad advice since I was standing on the roof's ledge at the time.

A student wanted to start after gymnastics. "Well how flexible are you?" asked the coach. "I can't come Tuesdays and Wednesdays."

I remember in one PE class I forgot my shorts and panicking, I just went straight to the lesson in my jocks. So that ended my career then and there.

The PE teacher took the students to the Rockies for a skiing trip. Unfortunately, he couldn't ski and it all went downhill.

The youth detention centre is starting to get the students to dance to the Hokey Pokey in gym class. They are hoping it will turn them around.

A PE Teacher was just asked by one of his students. "Who do you think are the smartest teachers at the school? The science or the maths teachers?" asked the student,

"The PE teachers, of course. Most of the time we are just having fun playing ball games, but we are getting paid the same as everyone else." He replied.

During gym class, this one student was just arguing the whole time.

"I won't do it! You can't make me do squat!"

I remember when the news flashed up that the school's gym teacher was just arrested for selling drugs to students. I was shocked, when did he become a gym teacher?

In health class, I learned the dangers of smoking cigarettes today. Thank God I switched to crack last week.

Did you hear about the orphan that was playing baseball? When the coach yelled "run home", he got lost.

My girlfriend asked me, "How many girls have you slept with?"

"11" I said.

"Wow, 11 that's a lot! You must have been a player," she said joking.

"Not really. I was their coach."

A young man started going to the gym and saw a fitness instructor.

"What machine should I use to impress the ladies the most?"

He asked.

"The ATM." He replied.

Why did the ghost join the football team?

He heard the coach say that they lacked team spirit.

I got kicked off the baseball team. The coach told me to steal third base and I did.

His daughter loved it but man he was pissed!!

Reading and Writing

An English teacher in a rural town asks her class to give a sentence using the words; defense, defeat and detail. A student answers, "Well, Miss. When me horse jumps defense, defeat go first, and detail goes last."

I am close friends with 25 letters of the alphabet, I don't know Y.

What do an English teacher and a judge have in common?
They both give sentences.

What do you say to an upset English teacher?
There, their, they're

Who was the genius that put the letter B in the word subtle?

What's the difference between a comma and a cat?
One has it's claws at the end of its paws. The other has a pause at the end of the clause.

What was Shakespeare's favorite pencil?
2B

An English teacher asked one of her students.
"Can you give me two pronouns?"
"Who me?"

What do you call an English teacher who corrects everyone's social media?
Insta-grammar

I ran into my old English teacher the other day.
"What's new?" I asked.
"An adjective", she answered.

Why did Jeffery Epstein's English teacher fail him?
Because he never finishes his sentences

I ran into my old English teacher the other day. I was so excited I ran up and said hi, but they didn't remember. I was devastated considering she said I was her favorite student and I was actually home-schooled.

I got dumped by an English teacher the other day for inappropriate use of the colon.

What do you get when you cross an English teacher with a software engineer?
A programmar.

What does an English teacher tell her students before an exam?
Metaphors be with you.

What does an English teacher drink?
Tequila mockingbird

What does an English teacher say when taking photos?
Smilie.

What does an English teacher have for breakfast?
Synonym rolls.

What does an English teacher tell their class?
Double negatives are a big NO-NO.

Did you hear about the English teacher that had anxiety?
It was past tense.

A teacher wrote on the whiteboard, 'I isn't had no fun in the holidays.'
"Ok class, what do I need to do to correct this?"
"Get a boyfriend or girlfriend miss, we don't judge."
Cried little Jimmy.

$$yx - x + z = 2$$
$$x + yx - z = \lambda$$
$$y + x + \lambda = \lambda$$

$$\sqrt{18 \cdot yz}$$

$$mc^2 = c\pi$$

$$E = mc = \pi n^2$$

$$\pi 2x = \frac{3tx}{1x - y}$$

Finger Counting

Two surfers who hadn't seen each other in ages were meeting up on the beach.

"Hey Brah, I haven't seen you in ages." the first surfer says.

"Yeah Brah, I wanted to study Marine Biology so I could learn more about the ocean." Says the second surfer.

"Really Brah?"

"Yeah Brah but it was too much math, there was a lot of Algae Brah."

Why was the calculus teacher bad at baseball?
He was good at fitting curves, not hitting them.

What is a Maths teacher's favorite salad?
Cos law.

Why does the average always end up in detention?
They are a mean statistic.

A biology teacher and a maths teacher get together and decide to make a plan to save the planet. They called it the Al-gor-ithm.

Why don't you pick fights with a maths teacher?
Because you are always outnumbered.

Why are maths textbooks miserable?
They are full of problems.

"Algebra is stupid, like seriously when will I ever need to know!" a student complains to the teacher.
"You will never need it, but the smart kids in class will." replies the teacher.

What is a maths teacher's favorite snake?
A Pi-thon.

What is a maths teacher favorite time of year?
Sum-mer.

What do maths teachers eat?
Square Meals.

Did you hear about the maths teacher that confiscated a calendar?
Their days were numbered.

Teacher: If you had 7 apples in 1 hand and 6 apples in another hand, what would you have?
Student: Huge hands

Who invented fractions?
Henry the 1/4th

Why did the maths teacher fire his gardener?
Because his garden was filled with square roots.
maths

How did the maths teacher propose to his girlfriends?
With a polynomial ring.

Why did the maths teacher send the cold students to the corner of the room?
Because it was 90^0.

My maths teacher told me I was an average student. I guess it was because I was always mean to him.

A maths student was really upset about their detention. It just didn't add up.

I got detention while learning about geometry, I really didn't enjoy the aftermath.

Chemicals that go bang

During a biology exam, a question was asked. 'Explain 3 positives about breast milk.'
Little Jimmy answered; contains all the vital nutrients, doesn't need heating, and has great packaging.

A biology teacher was asked to step in as a history teacher, and she did very well. The first thing she did was get the students to draw a picture of Abraham Lincoln and then label the parts.

High school was exactly like Darwin's theory, I wasn't selected for anything.

A student was up to the last question in his botany exam, but he couldn't finish it. He was stumped.

Why does getting a B for your biology practical make the class difficult?
Because a frog is easier to dissect.

How did the frogs feel about the biology class?
They were pithed.

What did the professor say to the biology student when their grade fell from A to F?
You're biodegraded.

Why aren't students allowed in the biologist canteen?
It's staph only.

What did the biology student call a microtome?
A very small, tiny book.

I made a joke in biology class, but no one laughed,
I think my thymine was off.

What do students who received a fail in biology get on their transcript?
A Bio-D-grade.

Why did the biologist student fail the practical?
Because the tutor was sternum.

During a biology lecture, the professor was giving a talk on sex cells and was talking about the high glucose levels found in semen. A new female student puts up her hand and asks, "Excuse me but are you talking about glucose? The same glucose that is found in sugar?"
"Yes, that is correct." answers the professor.

"Then how come it doesn't taste sweet?" she blurted out without thinking.

With embarrassment, she packs her things and makes for the door quickly.

"Oh, that is because the taste buds for sweetness are found on the tongue, not at the back of the throat." answers the professor.

I learnt today that the biggest organ is the human skin. I always thought it was in the town cathedral.

A biology teacher was teaching students about male anatomy. She was explaining the places and differences in the glands, testicles and epididymis and the function of the urethra.

"Miss, I thought that the testicles and the urethra were the same thing?"

"No there is vas deferens between the two."

My favorite topic about physics was displacement, it was straight to the point.

In Physics the more you know the less you know. You start with Classical Physics where you can't solve the three-bodied problem. Next, you learn the theory of relativity where we can't solve the two-body problem. In quantum mechanics, you can't solve the one-body problem and finally, with quantum electrodynamics, you don't even understand vacuums anymore.

A student was getting angry with his Physics Teacher.
He kept asking, "What is the unit for Power?"
The teacher kept saying, "Yes!"

A physics teacher was dealing with a student who was not only the heaviest but also the rudest brat he ever came across. The student would make fart noises, stealing other people's books and pens. In the last lesson, the kid leaned forward and unclipped a bra strap of the girl in front.
"That's it, I need to speak to you outside!" yells the physics teacher.
"Yeah, no worries," the fat kid replies with a smirk.
Outside the teacher has now lost all his anger and seems sincere.
"Look, buddy, I honestly think you have the most potential in the class, I'll show you."
He then throws the student off the balcony.

Two physicists students are studying for a final exam, one was quite nervous, so the other says to him, Don't worry about it, you are gonna be Feynman.

Where should a physics class be held?
On the edge of a cliff. Its where they have the most potential,

A student in a Physics Lecture just before the class finishes asks, "So what happened before the Big Bang?" "No time." Answers the professor

A physics teacher asked a student. "Do you understand Linear Motion?"
"It's really straightforward," he replies.

Why couldn't the physics teachers get along?
There was too much friction between them.

A physics exam had the following question.
'A young child weighing 15 kg is being held by a parent whose arms are 102cm long. The child is swinging at a revolution 0.75 cm/s and the parent lets go. How far could the child potentially travel?.'
The best answer written was 'To foster care.'

Physics Professor: "Ok class, is there anything else you wish to know before tomorrow's exam?"
Student: "Can you go over terminal velocity?"
Physics Professor: "No."
In science class I hated the energy topic, it was nothing but work.

A chemistry teacher asks her class, "Ok, class, what is the formula for water?"
Little Robbie raises his hand, "Miss, miss, it's H, I, J, K, L, M, N, O."
"No, Robbie, it's H2O."
"That's what I said."

Why was the chemist disappointed in her son's report card?
Because it reminded her of tetrafluoroethylene (2 C's and 4 F's).

A chemistry professor is starting her lecture but is having computer problems. She then asks her class, "Does anyone know how to unfreeze a computer?"
Jimmy puts his hand up nervously, "Um, miss, what is the melting point?"

During chemistry class, the experiment was a group activity, and the students had to weigh and accurately record approximately 20 grams. One student went to borrow a pen to write the result. As soon as he picked it up, another student grabbed the pen and yelled, "Bromine!"

The student just shrugged his shoulders and went back to the experiment. He was watching his classmate weigh the sample. She weighed 43 grams.

"You're getting a bit overweight there", he said.

She snapped, "None of your Bismuth!!"

A chemistry teacher was yelling at his students for not knowing any of the chemical symbols.

"Back in my day, I would know all the symbols and the masses."

"Back in your day sir, there were on 20 odd elements."

Student 1: Do you get zinc sulphate by mixing zinc and sulphate?

Student 2: I Zinc So

If you wake up in a science lecture, how do you know which class you're in?

- If it moves, it's biology.
- If it stinks, it's chemistry.
- If it doesn't work, it's physics.

My Chemistry teacher asked me to rank all the bonds. So I did;

1) Daniel Craig
2) Sean Connery
3) Roger Moore
4) George Lazenby
5) Timothy Dalton
6) David Nevin
7) Peirce Brosnan

To be a successful prospector you don't need to have a major in geology. You just need a miner.

Some students were going on an excursion to Mt. Fuji. One of the kids complained saying "This blows!"

During a field trip for the class Environmental Earth Sciences, the students were taken to a quarry that was full of sedimentary rocks. The field trip consisted of studying the different strata specimens. To be honest, it wasn't that interesting, it was just boring.

A geology student came back from Brazil. He went to his university professor and gave him a gift… a little bottle of dirt from the Amazon River.
"Thank you for the sediment" replied the professor.

A kid walks into his earth science class
"This class rocks!" he yells out.
"That's gneiss, too bad you are so schist at it," says the teacher.

Naughty College

What are the main things you learned in Organic Chemistry?
How to connect the dots and how to draw hexagons.

When Hamilton applies the principle of least action he wins a Nobel Prize, when I try, I fail my exam.

On a university notice board, a question was posed.
'What is 3 X 3'?
The engineer excitedly pulls out his slide rule and shuffles it back and forward and finally determines it is 8.99.
The statistician gets his computer out, creates a program, makes a bell curve, and comes up with an answer that is in the range of 8.98 to 9.02.
The philosopher smiles and writes, "What do you mean 3 X 3?"
The socialist was just happy that everyone was talking about it.
The ecologist turns around and mentions that it is a polyamorous dating ritual.
The medical student pipes up, you know it's 9, right? I know because I memorized it.

What university professors are the shadiest?
Biology professors have a lot of skeletons in their closets.

At a university, who oversees the finances of the biology department?
A buy-al-agist.

When I was at university, I found all the geology majors used to smoke a lot of weed. I am not surprised. They were a bunch of stoners.

Study tip for chemistry students;

● Don't drink water when studying; it decreases your concentration.

What's the difference between hospitality and chemistry class?
You do not want to lick the spoon after chemistry class

A student was up all night studying for his zoology exam, looking at all the rare endangered species around the globe and their locations. It was the last exam he had to do before he graduated. The next day, being summer, he walked into the auditorium ready for his exam with 300 hundred other students wearing his lucky shorts. He looked upon the stage and saw 8 platforms. On each platform, there was a bird with a sheet over it. You could only see the bottom of their legs and feet.

The professor gets on stage and explains. The students only get to look at that part of the animal. They then must describe the function of the feet; from there they must deduce the species and family names. The student looked complexed. He started sweating he had no idea. He started thinking of the injustice. It wasn't fair he had studied hard but did not have a clue. He started getting angrier and angrier until he reached a breaking point. Standing up he threw his books on the ground and yelled, "FUCK THIS!"

The professor was in a state of shock as the student was walking away.

"What's your name?!" he yelled after the student.

"Well look at my fucken legs and tell me what family I come from!!"

This chemistry professor had a new batch of students. They were awful, talking back, making smart-ass comments all the time, and rarely letting him finish a sentence.

During a practical class, they were all standing around his bench for a demonstration. In the centre of the table was a beaker with some orange liquid in it.

"Ok class, to be a good chemist, you have to be very observant and take notes of the smallest things," he said as he dipped his finger in the liquid. He then sucked on a finger.

"Ok class, please do as I did."

So, the students stuck a finger in the liquid, and then sucked.

"Ok class, what did you observe?"

"Oh, it's just dyed water. That was pointless." remarked one student.

"No, it tastes slightly salty," said another.

Sure enough, an argument started with the students. The professor then went back to his desk, grinning from ear to ear.

"Sir, why are you smiling?" asked a student.

"Well, if you were observant, you would have noticed that I put my pointer in the liquid but sucked on my pinkie. Meanwhile, you just all tasted my urine."

During university finals for chemistry, the very last question given to the students was:

'Is hell exothermic or endothermic? Discuss using theory.'

Most students spoke of the Molecular Theory of Particles in an excited state; when they have more energy, they expand and become gas or lose energy and become liquids, then solids.

One student took a different approach;

The first constant that is needed is mass, the actual mass of hell. This, unfortunately, is not constant as hell is not a closed system; souls are entering and leaving all the time. Hell, being hell would not allow many souls to escape, so it is safe to assume that the mass is constantly increasing.

How many souls are actually entering hell? If we take into account the world's religions, the vast majority of them believe in hell so those souls would go to hell. If we also look at the world's population. It is expanding in exponential growth. The rate of births is exceeding the rate of deaths. Thus, we can hypothesize that the rate of souls entering hell would also be increasing exponentially as well.

If you look at Boyles Law and the relationships between volume, pressure and temperature, we have to have to decide that either;

1. If hell's volume is not increasing or increasing slower than the number of souls entering, then hell must be exothermic. It will keep getting hotter until all hell breaks loose.
2. If hell's volume is increasing faster than the souls entering it, which would mean an overall energy loss, then hell would be endothermic and hell would indeed freeze over.

Which is it then?

A fellow student, Diana, had postulated to me in high school that she will only go on a date with me if hell freezes over. This was said to me 4 years ago. However, 2 nights ago, that date did occur. So now we definitely know that hell is endothermic.

On a side note, the existence of God was also proven as by the end of the night, she kept screaming, "Oh God, Oh God, Oh God!"

He received an A+.

What is smarter, a thermometer or a beaker?
The Thermometer is smarter, the beaker may be graduated but the thermometer has a lot of degrees.

An undergrad student was caught cheating in his physics exam. The professor was busy giving him a lecture.

"Do you realize the gravity of this situation?" He snapped

"That's why I cheated because I didn't!!!"

Four University friends had an end-of-year exam for chemistry on a Monday morning. They were also invited to the Women's Volleyball Grand Final at another university, in different state. Not wanting to miss the opportunity to mix with some ladies, the boys decide to drive six hours across the state, then leave early the next morning so they would have Sunday afternoon to study.

So, the four boys left on a merry old road trip. They got to the game, celebrated at the after-party and drank the night away. Come Sunday the boys were too hungover to drive back let alone study. They eventually made it back late Sunday night with no time to study. They hatched a plan, deciding to email their university lecture and beg for forgiveness. They explained that they had to help a sick aunt move house but when they were coming home, they got a flat tyre and being a small town, it took 24 hours to get the tyre. Can they please have an extension or re-sit? The professor replied and gave them another 3 days.

Three days later the boys came to sit the exam. The exam was going to be marked out of a hundred. They blitzed the first page which was simply looking up masses from the periodic table and worth 5 points. Then they turned the page and looked at each other in shock and horror.

The last page read "For 85 points each of you has to say which tyre and all the answers have to be the same"

What did the grad student define hydrophobic as?
A fear of utility bills.

When a geophysicist completes their doctorate, they are initiated into a knighthood. It is called the tectonic order.

Sexy Teachers

Why is that Gym teachers always date the English teachers?

A very muscular university student was studying biology and failing. In fact, he was failing everything and failing miserably. The older but still attractive lecturer decided to help him out and made him an offer. She invited him over for dinner and a night of passion. In return, she would help him pass all the science subjects.

That night, he goes to the professor's house and the pair of them have great sex for the next few hours. He then leaves and they don't speak about the night for the rest of the semester.

Come to the end of the semester he gets his grades, and he looks at them. He got an A for chemistry, an A for physics but completely fails biology. He goes to the professor for a chat.

"You see," she starts explaining to him. "You got an A in chemistry because it was definitely there. You got an A in physics because you knew how much force to use. But as for biology, I know have a carbon-based life form inside of me because of you."

What was the motto of a biology teacher who moonlighted as a prostitute?
Sex cells.

Why was the music teacher fired?
They court fingering A Minor

If porn has taught me anything detention isn't a punishment

Why is it fun to date teachers?
If you get it wrong, then they make you go again.

There was a senile old biology professor who would often get distracted and just start telling dirty jokes.
Several students got sick of this behavior and decided to walk out the next time he started.
The following lecture he started, "That reminds me, did you know there is currently a shortage of prostitutes in Holland?"
The group of disgruntled students closed their books and began walking out.
The professor called out to them, "Ladies and Gents, no need to rush, the next plane leaves at 7 in the morning."

What is the difference between a paratrooper and a paragraph?
You only need one paratrooper to satisfy an English teacher.

A geology professor was busy describing the Mariana Trench to the class. It was the deepest, coldest, most inhospitable place on the planet. His associate, Mariana walked in and told him not to talk about their date like that.

I finally slept with my English teacher!! Homeschooling is great!!

Dr. Smith was teaching her biology class at a prestigious high school when she noticed one of the students not paying attention.
"Rose, can you name the part of the human anatomy that under appropriate conditions will grow up to 6 times larger?"
Rose freezes for a second, then slowly a smirk crosses her face.
"Um, Miss? Isn't that an inappropriate thing to ask me? I find that very offensive and I think I will complain to my parents." Rose answered with a smirk.

Unphased by this uppity student's remarks, she turns to another student.

"Lexi, can you name the part of the human anatomy that under appropriate conditions will grow up to 6 times larger?"

"It's the pupil under dim light!" Lexi replied.

"Very well-done Lexi, thank you for that brilliant answer."

She then turns back to Rose.

"I have 3 things to say to you. Firstly, it is quite clear that you haven't been paying attention or doing your homework. Secondly, I think I will have a conversation with your parents about your dirty mind! Lastly Rose, one day, most likely soon, you will be very disappointed."

A lecturer is busy telling his physics students the philosophy of physics.

"So, if you think about it, maths is to physics what masturbation is to sex."

"Um, what your saying is without the attempt to explain the why of the universe, the search for deeper mathematical truth is lonely and pointless?" asks a student.

"No, what I am saying is, you will spend most of your undergrad just doing maths."

There was an English teacher that was sleeping with a student. The teacher was caught, charged, and thrown in jail. Meanwhile, the student waited and waited for her release. He sent letters all the time and when the teacher was finally released from jail the student ran straight up to her and asked her to marry him. The English teacher said no. She could never finish a sentence with a proposition.

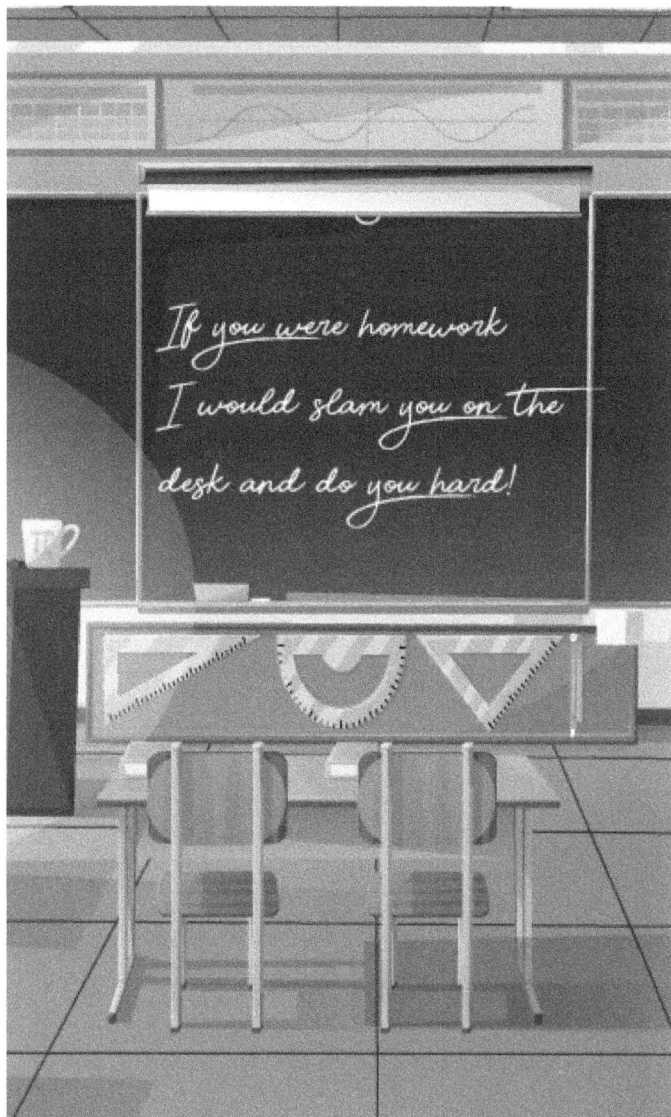

Pick Up Lines

Are you a physics teacher?
Because you got me harder than relativity.

Are you a maths textbook?
Because you are going to solve all my problems.

Are you a maths teacher?
Because my feelings have grown exponentially for you.

Are you a maths teacher?
Because you have one significant figure.

What is a maths teacher's favorite pickup line?
Can I evaluate you?

Do you teach astronomy?
Because you are out of this world.

Do you teach geometry?
Because every angle I look at you, your cute

Hey babes, I was in a history class we were learning about all the important dates, do you want to be one of them?

Hey babes, are we near the science class or is there chemistry between us?

Hey babes, I didn't know angels were allowed in public schools.

Hey babes, that lesson ran in perfect time with the bell and included classroom expectations, individual and group activities and high-order questions with a meaningful conclusion. Your lesson control is out of this world.

Hey babes, I am bad at studying so you can punish me as hard as you want.

Hey babes, you have the highest tolerance for organized chaos that I have ever seen.

Hey babes, would you like some hands on practice ?
Hey babes, do you want to sign the year book with that big pen of yours?

Hey babes, if you were a teacher I would go to every lesson of yours.

Hey babes, can you be my extracurricular activities?

Hey babes, you must be a perfect test score, because I want to bring you home and show you off to my parents.

Hey babes, you're so sweet I heard that they banned you from the school cafeteria.

Hey babes, life without you is like a broken pencil. Completely pointless.

A gym teachers pick up line:
- Drop and give me 69.
- I am going to help you feel the burn.
- Let's hit the shower, it's time for handball.
- Take a Lap.
- That's not rope burn.
- Wanna climb my rope?
- Hi, you really will do anything for an A.
- The pommel horse isn't the only horse in here, you should see what's in my pants.
- Think you're out of breath and sweaty now? Just wait a bit longer.
- I bet I can pick you up

A history teacher's pickup lines:

- I'm glad they repealed prohibition because I am drunk on you.

- Did you invent the airplane because we would be Wright together?

- Are you a president? Because you look like Babe-braham Lincoln.

- If you were from the Medieval period they would call you Sir Gagsalot.

- Did your dad work on the Manhattan project? Because you're the bomb.

- If I had to write a report card on you, I'd give you a hard f

Wow, I thought you were a student.

Wine on a school night? Well, let me pour you another.

I don't have a library card, but I still wouldn't mind checking you out.

I like my men the same way I like my bulletin boards. Bright, engaging, and well-informed.

If you were homework, I would slam you on the desk and do you hard.

If you were a multiple-choice question, I would only choose you.

Glossary

A

Accessibility – designing a task that allows everyone with specific needs the ability to complete it. Nothing to do with wheelchair access.

Accommodation – changing an assessment to suit specific needs. Nothing to do with hotels.

Accountability – able to pay all your bills and do your taxes.

Accreditation - something you do online.

Active Learning – in theory, it is where learners build their understanding of what is being taught. In practice- "nah this is too hard."

Adaptative Learning – goes at the speed of the learner. In most cases, don't expect 50% of the curriculum to get finished.

Added Value – unfortunately some students will never do this for society.

ADDIE – shorthand for the death adder snake

Adult Learning – if porn is anything to go by, this is about sex education.

Aptitude Test – how well you can separate and group, squares and circles.

Andragogy – expect adults to be adults in the classroom, given a fancy name to make someone else feel smart.

Appraisal – only ever happens when you've been very naughty.

Assessment as Learning – quizzes or exams to see how the kids are doing. Someone once again giving something a fancy name to sound more intelligent.

B

Behaviorism – the belief that behavior is caused by external stimuli but sometimes no matter what the stimuli are, the student will often leave you scratching your head and thinking "What the fuck?"

Benchmarking – making sure the non-athletic students know where to sit during the big game.

Bias – when you pick your favorite student to get the A+ (which of course never happens).

Bibliography – a line graph of bibles.

Bilingual – when your tongue plays with both sexes.

Blended Learning - hospitality class teaching students not to put their fingers into the blender.

Blended Learning - deep insight and breakdown of the theatrical masterpiece 'Blended' starring Adam Sandler and Drew Barrymore.

Bloom's Taxonomy - a tax on the number of plants you have flowering at a specific time.

Brainstorming – what you desperately try to do when your lesson totally shits itself and you want to get the class under control again.

Bulletin Board - the start of all the staff room gossip.

C

Case Study – my agriculture class.

Chat room – the place where you should never have a bitch about your colleagues or students.

Chunking – what happens after a big night of drinking and then you eat a kebab from Abdul's at 2 am.

Class exercises – In no way at all should you get students to do book work then either do push-ups, sit-ups or Kegel exercises.

Classroom Set-up – changing the room and desks around to make sure Little Jimmy is away from his friends to stop him from talking. Then realizing that he is now just shouting across the room instead.

Cognitive Load Theory – keep learning more information until you end up with a migraine.

Cognitive Science – the study of thought. In essence, the only study studying itself.

Cognitivism – a word I got taught at university that if you throw this into a sentence you seem smart.

Collaborative learning – stealing someone's work.

Competency-Based Learning – proving you can do something before moving on. Hence why most drummers read at a 4th grade level.

Comprehension – this is what happens when you have taught a fantastic and engaging lesson and then you go to check for understanding and you realize not one student has a fucking clue what you were talking about.

Computer-assisted learning – the class in which you must constantly say can you stop playing games please. However, I do get impressed because the students are always able to hack the education's security settings and then teach their friends and it takes weeks before the staff find out what's going on.

Constructivism – In theory, where students are meant to be constructing knowledge through social interactions. In practice, a few good kids get together and do the work and the rest want to be spoon-fed answers.

Context – when someone in prison sends a message.

Constructed Response – an answer that you gave them in many steps.

Counselor – when a student tells you something and you think, 'This is above my pay grade' then you palm them off to this person.

Curriculum – the stable be-all and end-all of what is meant to be taught in the classroom, which constantly changes as someone has to justify their jobs and affects thousands of teachers every year.

D

Deadline – the final date which constantly changes when a piece of work is due.

Deep Learning – having sex with a guy who has a big long dick.

Diagnostic test – what you give to a student to see how dumb he really is.

Distance Learning – learning from very far away. The main advantage is that you never have to be in the same room as smelly children.

Diversity – a city full of divers.

E

E–learning – using an e-cigarette for the first time.

Electronic Discussion board – 90% of the time it is as boring as bat shit but every so often you get an angry student abusing another student for not completing a part of their group assignment.

Employable skills – skills that are transferred from the classroom to the workplace. Like not telling the teacher to 'fuck off', it is not a wise move to do this to your boss either.

Essay – where students read something online, highlight it, copy it, paste it and then the clever ones change the format before handing it in.

Evaluation – judging how stupid the kids are.

Evidence – let's be honest, you only keep this because parents often think their kids are brilliant and you need proof to show that their beloved little Jimmy is a dumb ass.

Exercise – something that the teachers in the PE department are never short of doing.

External examiners – generally retirees that have nothing better to do than give themselves a minuscule amount of power.

F

Facilitator – the person who is ultimately responsible when the lesson/seminar turns to shit.

Feedback – what you give to a student to help improve grades. 'Better luck next time' or 'Keep trying' is not good feedback.

Fieldwork – When a teacher organizes an outdoor activity to a beach or cove to study marine life. This includes alignment of the activity to the curriculum, creating a workbook, creating risk assessments for activities, hiring the bus, collecting money and permission slips from parents, and monitoring student medical advice and first aid. Then during the activity, you watch little Jimmy and friends moon people from the bus, smoke in the public toilets and jump off the rocks to try to land on the dolphins.

Final Assessment – this entry speaks for itself.

Flowcharts – a graphical representation of a sequence of instructions or operations. IT guys and engineers do this very well; education administrators try to make it simple but also include every possible scenario to try and simplify it but turn it into convoluted crap.

Formative assessment – a simple quiz or pop test to tell you how well the kids are going. Another example of someone in education making a simple concept into a confusing one by changing and adding complicated terms and getting paid thousands of dollars to do it and pretending they are intelligent at the same time.

G

Grading – gives a student an overall mark and ultimately chooses their grade based on behaviour.

Grading rubric – what was straightforward in the 90's has become complex and convoluted, and open to huge amounts of interpretation which now allows teachers to get away with grading a student on personal opinions

Group assessment – where one student generally does 90% of the work, the others do bits and pieces, and little Johnny will once again do fuck all but will still pass because it is based on the group's overall mark. A clever way to lower your class's fail rate without doing any actual teaching.

Guidelines – the first thing the teachers try to read and see how they can work around them to keep doing what they want.

H

Halo effect – the bias to judge a student on previous favorable or unfavorable impressions, in education you do not say the 'asshole' effect because we do not speak negatively about students.

Handout – when you really can't be assed to teach that lesson.

I

Independent learners – the easiest kids to teach, why can't they all be like this?

Independent reading – the best part about being an English teacher is if you give up on teaching for the rest of the lesson, all you need to do to fill in time is resort back to independent reading.

Individual differences – unique characteristics of individuals and their ability to learn. What every teacher tries to cater to, but really can't unless you have a class size of 8 or 9 students.

Initiation phase – the hazing at a frat house.

Inquiry-based learning – when you give students a problem to solve and then have to give them every step and answer to solve that problem.

Instructional support – the talk you get when you do something wrong.

Intellectual property rights – when an employer tries to steal your ideas.

Interest groups – people who have no business in your classroom but want to question your actions.

Internet – teaching young boys about sex and porn for the last 30 years.

Intranet – poor persons internet.

J

Journal writing- about from a few weird folks who write down their dreams or the odd English teacher does anyone still do this?

Just-in-time-learning – the quick lesson the day before the final assessment when you think, "SHIT, I haven't taught that!" and give the students a crash course on it.

K

Key skills – mathematics.

Key skills - unfortunately critical thinking is no longer one.

Kolb's learning cycle – the push bike that Kolb used to help get rid of excess energy from students.

L

Laboratory-based education – burning pens in a Bunsen burner or throwing sodium into water.

Lateral thinking – something that is becoming increasingly rare.

Learning and Teaching strategy- what you use to try and justify your job or actions.

Learning Centers – someone trying to sound smart while describing their school or classroom.

Learning Contract- what you create at the beginning of the year with your students to try and convince them to behave well. Lasts for all 4 seconds.

Learning Logs – good students will use these, the rest will either rip pages out to send notes or just draw dicks.

Learning Objective – what you tell the students about what they are going to learn. E.g. If you are teaching a lesson about Mars, it should be pretty fucken obvious that your teaching them about Mars, but no sometimes you will have to actually tell them that it is a lesson about Mars.

Learning Outcome – apparently you have to tell the students when they have learned something.

Lifelong learning – unfortunately not what everyone is.

M

Managed Learning Environment – no windows, posters, colors, coloring in pencils crayons, scissors metal rulers or anything else that can be a distraction.

Mapping competence – able to get somewhere without a GPS.

Mentor – splinter from the Teenage Mutant Ninja Turtles.

Meta-Analysis -

Meta–cognition -

Meta–competence -

Meta-skill – how do you sound smarter when talking about education? Randomly throw the word Meta in front of everything.

Minimal competencies – breathing.

Mission Statement- fashionable in the '80s now a pointless must-have.

Model answer – when a model tries to answer a question. Eg

" I personally believe that U. S. Americans are unable to do so because, uh, some people out there in our nation don't *have* maps and, uh, I believe that our education, like such as in South Africa and, uh, the Iraq, everywhere like such as, and I believe that they should—our education over *here* in the *U. S.* should help the U. S., uh, or, should help South Africa and should help the Iraq, and the Asian countries, so we will be able to build up our future, for our children." *Miss Teen USA pageant 2007 – Caitlin Upton*

Module – a section of a rocket.

Monitoring achievement – every time a politician takes credit for something and publicizes it.

Motivation content – nudes or memes.

N

Networking – how to get a promotion.

Norm referencing - when you talk about a student who isn't classified as special needs, behavioral, challenged or LBQT.

O

Objective test – if your potential partner is attractive enough.

Open book examination- letting the students bring in answers to an exam. It will still not be able to help some students.

Online Learning – when you're told to do your own research and then get criticized and called a conspiracy theorist because you did your own research.

Open learning materials – computer and internet.

Open-ended questions – a question that lets you see how well you manipulated them.

Oral skills – how I assess my partners.

P

Pedagogy – the art and science of teaching which translates to a pseudo-science and the art of surviving.

Peer assessment – getting an A because you're popular.

Peer learning – cheating.

Performance criteria – how fast your car can go.

Performance indicator – how much money you spent on the engine.

Personal development plan – only for losers.

Personal tutor – unfortunately I never had sex with mine.

Phonemes – when you're an enemy over the phone (Facebook, Snapchat etc.) but civil to someone in public.

Plagiarism – never hand in your professor's paper and try to pass it off as your own, always check the authors first.

Portfolio – something you spend hundreds of hours creating for someone else to review in 30 secs and it never gets looked at again.

Positive Feedback – "You're fucken useless" is not an example.

Posters – something for the students to draw dicks on or get free blu tac from.

Problem-based learning – a more adept name for inquiry learning, it is just full of problems.

Product of learning- a 'yes person' who cannot critically think but will always pay their taxes.

Q

Quality assurance – an excuse for your peers to check in on you, then your line manager and finally some stranger from head office.

Quality control – there isn't any.

Question bank – having a supply of questions you can throw at the students when your lesson finishes early or when you run out of other ideas.

R

Range – how far you can shoot.

Record of achievement – the pretty stuff you put on your resume.

Redeemable failure – a nice kid that just fucked up, so you decide to give them another chance.

References – what you need to stop getting sued.

Reflection – what you see in the mirror.

Regional networks – the friends you need to get a promotion in head office.

Reliability – that booty call you can always ring when no one else is around.

Reports – the piece of paper which some students are terrified of.

Review – how critics make a living.

Role play – kinky times in the bedroom.

Rubric – a kid's toy.

S

Scaffolded instruction – what teachers have been doing for centuries but suddenly someone renames it and gets a bigger paycheck.

Software - when you wear something so tight you can't get an erection.

Self-assessment – telling yourself you are a legend over and over again.

Standards – the more you drink the less you have.

Study group – at university it was the perfect opportunity to sleep with other people in the subject.

Study skills – skills I picked up by having lots of fun in the study groups.

Summary -when you add the weight of all the Marys in your class together.

Surface learning – learning just enough so that you can bullshit your way through job interviews.

Synchronous communication – a perfectly working gearbox.

T

Taxonomy – trying to get out of paying taxes and keeping your own money.

Teamwork – a gangbang.

Theis – when writing one remembers "Bullshit baffles minds", so if you confuse your teacher, you will get an 'A'.

Time management – something teachers have in abundance but no matter how good you are you will still end up marking at home.

Transcript – something teachers hold over students to get them to pass but is what no employer ever looks at.

Tutor – if porn has taught me anything tutors will have sex with anyone and will get you a pass grade.

V

Validity – no matter how stupid the student is you still have to make him feel like a valuable member of the class.

Value – no matter how hard you try some students will still not add any value to society.

Video streaming - the unofficial babysitter of the class when the teacher has run out of energy or patience to keep teaching.

Virtual field trip – somehow little Johnny still got caught smoking behind the public toilets.

Vocational courses – you get to play with cool toys and make shit.

W

Webmaster - the best spiderman impersonator.

Weighting – what boxes do just before a fight.

Widening access – making the classroom doors bigger so really obese people can also be taught in the classroom. Education is for everyone.

Work experience – having sex with the pre-service teacher in the printing room is a great experience.

Word length – measuring in cm's how long a word is.

Workload – how much stress your back can take because you are busy doing all the work for all the lazy bastards in your department.

Work placement – the desk they tell you to sit at for the next 20yrs of your life.

Socrates Misquote
"A totally Free Adult Joke eBook at:

https://www.unconventionalpublishing.com.au

Nawty Jokes for You; Adults Only Edition."

AUTHOR'S NOTE

Thank you for taking the time to read this book. I hope you had just as many laughs as I did in writing this book. If you did enjoy reading this, please leave a review that would be greatly appreciated, and would help me out immensely.

Free Adult Jokes Book

You can also find another free joke book on the company's website, one that is not for sale, one that is not for the faint-hearted, and one that can be considered a bit risqué and politically incorrect. Consider this a gift for taking the time to purchase and read my book but be warned, only download it if you are not easily offended.

www.unconventionalpublishing.com.au

If you want to see any other professions being roasted or want a particular joke on a shirt, please visit our website and let us know.

Kind Regards

Shane Van

Other Great Books in the series

www.ingramcontent.com/pod-product-compliance
Lightning Source LLC
Chambersburg PA
CBHW041819090426
42811CB00009B/1033